The Alamo

CORNERSTONES OF FREEDOM™

SECOND SERIES

Tom McGowen

Children's Press®
A Division of Scholastic Inc.
New York • Toronto • London • Auckland • Sydney
Mexico City • New Delhi • Hong Kong
Danbury, Connecticut

Photographs © 2003: Arkansas History Commission: 8; Art Resource, NY/Donne Bryant: 41; Brown Brothers: 7, 16, 26; Corbis Images: 6, 10, 44 bottom left (Bettmann), 11 left, 45 bottom left (Michael Freeman), cover top, 23, 45 center left (David Muench), 27 (Lee Snider); Daughters of the Republic of Texas Libary at the Alamo: 20, 36; Hulton|Archive/Getty Images: 30, 31; Nick Romanenko: 17, 18 top; North Wind Picture Archives: cover bottom, 5 top, 9, 13, 22, 25, 40, 44 top left, 44 top right; State Preservation Board, Austin, Texas: 11 right, Stock Montage, Inc.: 12 left, 19, 45 center right; Texas State Library/Archives Commission: 3, 5 bottom, 12 right, 14, 15, 24, 28, 29, 32, 33, 34, 35, 38, 39, 44 bottom right, 45 top, 45 bottom right; The Image Works/Bob Daemmrich: 21; University of Texas at Austin, Center for American History/Prints and Photographs Collection: 18 bottom.

XNR Productions:Map on page 4

    Library of Congress Cataloging-in-Publication Data
McGowen, Tom.
  The Alamo / Tom McGowen.
    p. cm. — (Cornerstones of freedom. Second series)
  Summary: Discusses historical events surrounding the Battle of the
Alamo, including the roles played by Mexican General Santa Anna and
Americans Stephen F. Austin, Jim Bowie, Davy Crockett, Sam Houston,
and others.
  Includes bibliographical references and index.
   ISBN 0-516-24208-3
   1. Alamo (San Antonio, Tex.)—Siege, 1836—Juvenile literature.
[1. Alamo (San Antonio, Tex.)—Siege, 1836. 2. Texas—History—
Revolution, 1835–1836.] I. Title. II. Series.
F390 .M524 2003
976.4'03—dc21

                        2002009033

1 2 3 4 5 6 7 8 9 10 R 12 11 10 09 08 07 06 05 04 03

BLUE-COATED SOLDIERS were swarming over the fort's wall. An uproar of shouts, curses, screams of pain, and bangs of muskets being fired filled the air. The fort's defenders knew the leader of the enemy forces had ordered that they were to be killed to the last man. With muskets, knives, and tomahawks, they prepared to die fighting!

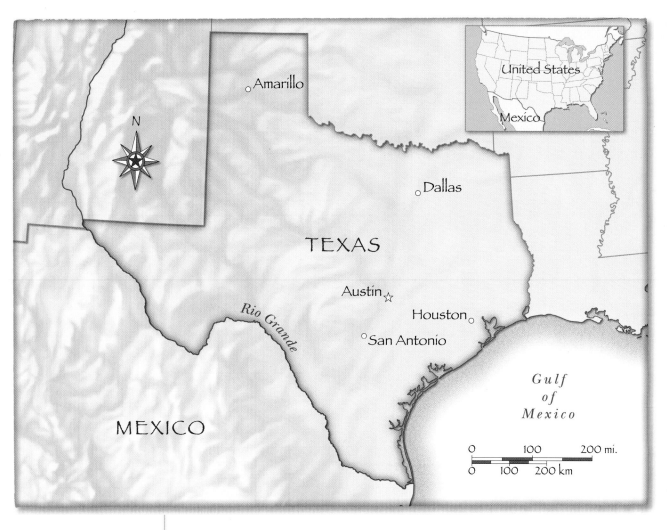

Map of modern day Texas and the Rio Grande

Some three centuries ago, Spanish explorers crossed over the Rio Grande (Great River) from Mexico, entering a region that was the home of many Native American tribes. These tribes called this land Tejas. In time, Tejas was claimed by Spain as part of Mexico, which was a province of the Spanish Empire.

In 1718 some Mexican missionaries went into Tejas to build a mission, a place where they could live and teach

Catholicism to the Native Americans. The mission was built in 1724 on a branch of a river the Spanish explorers had named the San Antonio (Saint Anthony), so it became known as the Misión San Antonio de Valero. It consisted of a small church, a **monastery,** and a rectangular courtyard inside 12-foot (3.6-meter) high, 3-foot (0.9-m) thick walls, with rows of small rooms built along the walls' inner sides.

By 1793 most of the Native Americans living in the area had been converted to Catholicism, so there was no longer

An early 19th–century view of San Antonio from the San Antonio River

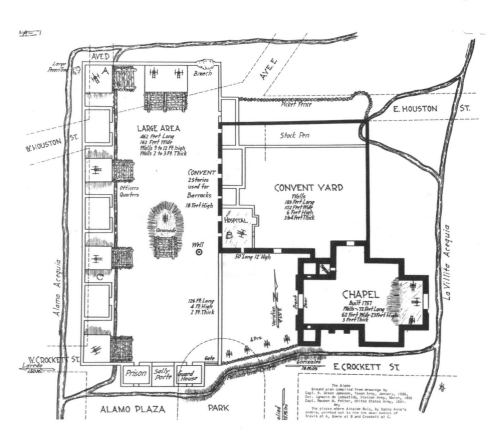

Diagram of the Alamo, showing where it once stood in relation to present-day San Antonio

any need for a mission. However, a town called San Antonio de Bexar had grown up outside the mission, and a company of Spanish cavalry was sent to defend the town against Native American raids. The soldiers decided to turn the mission into a barracks, where they could live and keep their horses. Because there were many cottonwood trees growing in the area, the barracks became known as the *Alamo,* the Spanish word for cottonwood.

In 1810 a movement began in Mexico for independence from Spain. For the next eleven years a revolutionary war raged throughout the land. By the end of 1821 Mexico had won its independence. In 1824 it became a **republic,** with a constitution based to some extent on the United States Constitution.

San Antonio in the early 19th century

Miguel Hidalgo, a Catholic priest, began Mexico's war of independence against Spain by calling for Mexico's native population to rebel.

"TEXAS FEVER" AND TOUGH FRONTIERSMEN

Tejas was part of the Mexican republic but it was still a **frontier** region—wide-open country, with few people, few communities, and enormous amounts of rich farm and ranch land. For this reason Americans found Tejas attractive and

Poor Americans living in crude cabins in Arkansas wrote "GTT" on their cabin doors and headed off to Texas.

settled there, becoming Mexican citizens. The native Mexican citizens living in Tejas spoke Spanish and pronounced it *tey-has,* with the *h* having a soft, scratchy sound, somewhat like a whispered *k.* They called themselves Tejanos *(tey-hanos).* The Americans couldn't quite make the soft, scratchy sound, so they called their new land Texas and themselves Texians.

The desire to move to Texas captured the imagination of more and more Americans and became known as "Texas Fever." Many poor Americans living in crude cabins in the southeastern part of the United States would scratch the letters G-T-T on their cabin door and leave. "GTT" stood for

★ ★ ★ ★

"Gone to Texas." By 1830 there were about twenty thousand Americans living in Texas, and this alarmed the Mexican government. A law was passed forbidding any more **immigration** from the United States. This angered most Texians. They believed it was Americans who had made Texas into the free, prosperous land it was.

Texians split into two political parties. One was known as the War Party, sometimes called the War Dogs. Many War Party members were frontiersmen who had come from American frontier regions, where much of the land was wilderness. There were often bloody wars and battles between the frontier Americans and Native American

A peril faced by wagon trains on the frontier was attacks by Native Americans

Early frontiersmen like this one were rugged adventurers who loved hunting and the outdoors.

AMERICAN FRONTIERS IN 1830

In 1830 the United States consisted of twenty-four states and several frontier regions—the Michigan Territory (today's Michigan and Wisconsin), the Arkansaw [sic] Territory (Arkansas and part of Oklahoma), the Florida Territory, and a vast unorganized territory that included many of today's midwestern states. The United States also claimed land in what was known as the Oregon Country (present-day Oregon, Washington, and Idaho).

tribes, who resented these frontiersmen pushing into their land. Many frontiersmen were tough, violent men, who seemed to like fighting and taking risks, and were not at all reluctant to kill someone they felt was an enemy. The War Party wanted to take Texas away from Mexico and make it part of the United States. They were willing to fight a revolutionary war to do this, if necessary.

A typical War Party member was James Bowie, who came to San Antonio from Louisiana in 1828. Bowie had a reputation as a knife-fighter. He had killed several men with a special knife, called the Bowie knife, that was invented by his brother,

10

* * * *

Rezin Bowie. In 1831, Bowie married a Mexican woman and soon became an important man in San Antonio.

Another War Party member was Sam Houston, who ran away from home when he was fifteen and lived on the frontier among the Cherokee people as a young man. Later, he

Jim Bowie

Bowie knife

THE FAMOUS BOWIE KNIFE

Jim Bowie's brother, Rezin, made Jim's knife by hand. The blade was said to be 9 inches (almost 23 cm) long and one and one-half inches (3.81 cm) wide. It had a sharp point and a razor-like bottom edge.

★ ★ ★ ★

became an officer in the United States Army and fought in a war against the Creek tribes of Alabama. At the age of thirty he was elected to the United States Congress as a representative from Tennessee. In 1827 he was elected governor of Tennessee. He resigned the governorship in 1829 and moved to Texas, where he became a trader and traded with the Native Americans.

Still another War Dog was William Travis, nicknamed "Buck," who came to Texas in 1831. It was rumored that he had murdered a man in South Carolina.

Sam Houston played an important role in the history of Texas.

William Travis, commanded the forces at the Alamo

STRIVING FOR PEACE, PREPARING FOR WAR

The other Texian group was known as the Peace Party. These Texians wanted to try to get along with the Mexican government. They hoped to make Texas a separate Mexican state and to gain all the rights of statehood.

In 1833, Antonio López de Santa Anna, a Mexican general, became president of Mexico. He had played a big part in making Mexico a republic, and in 1829, when Spain tried to reconquer Mexico, he led the Mexican army to a victory that forced the Spanish to leave. This made him a great hero to the people of Mexico. The members of the Peace Party thought he might listen to their ideas and agree to make Texas a Mexican state. Peace Party leaders drew up a list of requests and sent them to President Santa Anna. The man who carried them to the president was a Texian named Stephen F. Austin.

Stephen F. Austin was born in Virginia. He came to Texas in 1821 with his father, Moses Austin. The Mexican government had given Moses a grant of land on the Brazos River to start an American colony. But Moses died in 1821, and Stephen took over the work of establishing the colony of

From 1833 to 1855, general Santa Anna ruled Mexico eleven seperate times.

Stephen Austin made many diplomatic trips to Mexico on behalf of Texas, and did his best to prevent war with Mexico.

three hundred American families. Both the Texians and the Mexican government held him in high regard. He seemed to be the perfect person to convince the Mexican president to make Texas a state.

At first, Santa Anna seemed to listen to Austin. Then, however, Austin was thrown into jail, accused of plotting to make Texas part of the United States. He stayed there for a year and a half.

It soon began to look as if President Santa Anna wanted to be more powerful than a mere president. By 1834 he had abolished the Mexican constitution, gotten rid of all government officials who disagreed with him, and become Mexico's **dictator**—sole ruler with total power.

Most Texians and many Tejanos soon believed that with Santa Anna in power, they would have no freedom at all. It seemed that the War Party was right: the only choice was to break away from Mexico. Even Stephen F. Austin, who had finally been let out of jail, now favored a revolutionary war. "We must defend our rights, ourselves, and our country by force of arms," he declared.

In September of 1835, Santa Anna sent a small army of four hundred men into Texas, commanded by his own brother-in-law, General Martín de Cós. Cós was to go to San Antonio, gather the four hundred Mexican troops stationed there, and begin forcing the Texians to give up all their weapons. Santa Anna intended to keep the Texians from being able to start a revolution.

However, the revolution started before Cós even arrived. The commander of the Mexican troops in San

General Martín de Cós commanded the Mexican forces sent by Santa Anna to prevent a revolution in San Antonio.

Antonio sent a small force to the Texian town of Gonzales to take away a cannon the town owned. The Texians knew the soldiers were coming and formed a small army of about three hundred men. On October 2, when the Mexican troops arrived, the Texians attacked them, firing a

A frontiersman wearing deerskin coat and breeches and coonskin cap

blast from their cannon. The Mexicans retreated. The Texas War of Independence had begun!

Texians began to hurry to Gonzales from all over Texas. Stephen F. Austin, Sam Houston, Jim Bowie, and William Travis all arrived. The little army chose Stephen F. Austin as its general, even though he had never been a soldier. Jim Bowie was made a colonel. Bowie's wife and children had died in a terrible epidemic of the disease called typhus, which had swept through Texas, and he now seemed to have only one purpose in life—to fight to make Texas free. On October 12 this little army set out to capture San Antonio from the Mexican troops there.

These men called themselves "the Army of the People," but they were nothing like a real army. They had no discipline, the enforced obedience to rules necessary to run an army. They argued with their officers, often refused to obey orders, and generally did as they pleased. They had no uniforms. Many wore frontiersmen's clothing—deerskin coats and **breeches** and coonskin caps. A coonskin cap was made of a raccoon **pelt,** with the bushy, striped tail hanging down behind. Other men dressed in the typical clothing worn in cities and towns of that time.

Their main weapons were flintlock muskets and rifles, both of which fired a one-ounce (28-gram) lead ball. The musket had a range of about one hundred yards (90 m), and the rifle, 200 yards (180 m). They had to be reloaded after each shot. Reloading was slow and complicated, and all the

Musket and lead balls were the primary weapons used by the defenders of the Alamo.

POWDER, BALL, AND RAMROD

To load a flintlock musket or rifle, some gunpowder was sprinkled onto the firing pan and then the rest was poured into the **barrel.** A ball was pushed down onto the powder with a long rod, called a ramrod. All this took about fifteen seconds.

Rifle, ramrod, and bayonet (above) and pistols and tomahawk (below)

Texians had "backup" weapons with which to defend themselves if they couldn't get their gun loaded in time. Most men carried large knives, often copies of the famous Bowie knife. Many also carried a tomahawk, a Native American weapon that was a sharp-bladed hand ax with a long handle.

18

A view of the walls and church at the Alamo, long after the famous battle took place there

THE BATTLE OF SAN ANTONIO

On November 1 the Army of the People reached San Antonio. It had grown along the way, picking up more Texians and also a number of Tejanos willing to fight against other Mexicans in order to make Texas free. But General Cós was in San Antonio with more than eight hundred men, and he had repaired the Alamo and converted it to a fort. Platforms of earth had been built at places along the wall and cannons mounted on them. Wooden fences had been put in front of

Men of the Army of the People volunteer to attack the Mexican army in San Antonio.

some walls to slow down attackers while soldiers fired on them from above. For the Texians to make a direct attack would be suicide.

General Austin decided on a **siege,** surrounding the town with soldiers so that no one could get in or out. When the Mexican soldiers ran out of food, they would have to surrender.

As the siege began, the men who had been selected to govern Texas began working on a number of problems. They decided that Texas needed a regular army and a real general. Sam Houston had been an officer in the U.S. Army, so they appointed him general. They also decided to send Stephen F. Austin to Washington, D.C., to ask for help from the United States government. He was replaced as commander of the force in San Antonio by Edward Burleson, who had been a colonel in the Tennessee **militia.**

The siege of San Antonio dragged on for more than a month. The size of the Army of the People grew to about 550

Texas revolution cannon, used in the battle of 1836, on display at the Alamo

CANNON AT THE BATTLE OF SAN ANTONIO

A cannon was a large gun mounted on a two-wheeled wooden carriage. Cannons of 1835 fired solid iron balls or hollow metal balls filled with bullets or chunks of scrap metal. They could fire only about twice a minute.

men as volunteers from the United States came to help them. They now also had some cannons. On December 5, 1835, they launched an attack.

For several days they fought their way through the town, steadily losing men to cannon fire and musket balls. But General Cós's force in the Alamo was out of food and nearly out of ammunition. On December 9, Cós surrendered. The Texians allowed him to march back to Mexico with what was left of his army.

The men of the Army of the People were convinced they had defeated Mexico and set Texas free. The army broke up as many men returned to their homes. They were sure there would be no more trouble from the Mexican government.

Santa Anna in military uniform

They were wrong. General Santa Anna decided he had to personally do something about these rebellious Texians. In late December he assembled an army of Mexico's best troops and prepared to march on Texas. He made it known that he intended harsh punishment for those who had dared rebel against him. He was going to wipe them out!

There were still eighty-eight men of the Army of the People in San Antonio, under the command of Colonel James Neill. On January 19, Colonel Jim Bowie showed up with thirty men sent by General Houston. Colonel Bowie believed San Antonio was the "key" to the rest of Texas and the Mexicans should be prevented from capturing it. San Antonio could not be taken without gaining control of the Alamo, so Bowie and Neill decided the Alamo must be held. The Alamo still had twenty-one cannons in place, and Neill and his men had worked to strengthen it further. Bowie and Neill agreed to use it as a fort, as the Mexicans had done.

23

Although Davy Crockett first became famous as a frontiersman in Tennessee, he loved Texas. Shortly before the battle at the Alamo, he told his daughter in a letter, "I would rather be in my present situation than elected to a seat in Congress for life."

On February 3, William Travis, now a lieutenant colonel, arrived with thirty more men. And on February 8 another American frontiersman who had been seized by "Texas Fever" showed up—the famous Davy Crockett of Tennessee.

Davy Crockett ran away from his Tennessee home when he was thirteen years old and began working as a wagon driver. Eventually, he became a farmer and tried to settle down. But at the age of twenty-seven he enlisted in the U.S. Army to fight in the war against the Creek tribes. Later, he was elected to the U.S. Congress three times as a representative from Tennessee. Like many frontiersmen, he seemed to enjoy a fight, even a fistfight, just for the fun of it. In a tale Crockett

Warriors of the Native American Creek tribe

25

David Crockett, dressed in a suit he would have worn while serving as representative from Tennessee to the U.S. Congress

claimed to have written himself, he said he had once been nearly "spoiled" (turned rotten) because he hadn't had a fight in ten days! Now he had come to help the Texians fight and had brought a small group of men with him.

THE COMING OF SANTA ANNA

The little force in the Alamo knew a Mexican army would soon arrive. They kept watch and waited. The days of February crept by. On February 14, Neill left to go to his wife, who was desperately ill. Travis and Bowie were now in command.

Early on the morning of February 23, 1836, most Tejano citizens of San Antonio began leaving the town. They had learned that Santa Anna's army was only a few miles away. However, a number of Tejanos stayed on to help the Texians defend the Alamo.

The highest place in San Antonio was the bell tower of the San Fernando church. The soldier on duty there had orders to ring the bell if he saw the Mexican army approaching. At about ten o'clock that morning, the bell suddenly began clanging furiously.

San Fernando Church bell tower in San Antonio, where a soldier was stationed to watch for the Mexican Army

Colonel Travis rushed up the tower stairs, followed by other Texians. But when they reached the top and peered toward the hilly country to the south, they saw nothing.

27

The uniform of the Mexican army can be seen in this copy of a painting entitled *The Death of Lieutenant Dickinson*.

However, the sentry swore he had seen a mass of soldiers coming toward San Antonio.

Travis asked for volunteers to ride out and take a look. Two men set out. Reaching the top of a hill about a mile and a half (2.4 kilometers) from San Antonio, they pulled their horses to a sudden stop. On the flat ground beyond

the hill they saw what they believed to be some fifteen hundred Mexican cavalrymen, the sharp points of their lances gleaming in the sunlight. This was the advance-guard of Santa Anna's army.

The two Texians turned their horses and galloped furiously back to the town. Travis and others watching from the church tower knew they must have seen the enemy.

Travis began yelling orders, and San Antonio became a whirlwind of activity. Men went streaming through the streets toward the Alamo, some bringing their wives or families with them. Travis sent messengers galloping out to the nearest towns, asking for immediate help. Jim Bowie and a party of soldiers went through the town ransacking every empty house for food. They found ninety baskets of dried corn, which they carried into the fort. Another group of soldiers rounded up thirty head of cattle and herded them into the Alamo. Soon there was enough food for several weeks. Water was no problem, as the Alamo had its own well inside the walls.

WERE THERE ANY CHILDREN IN THE ALAMO?

The baby daughter of two Texians, the baby son of a Texian and his Mexican wife, the five children of a Tejano couple, and other Tejano children were in the Alamo with their parents when the Mexicans attacked.

29

At about three o'clock, as the last of the Texians were entering the fort, the Mexican army entered San Antonio. Unlike the scruffy Texians, these men wore uniforms copied from those of the French Army that had conquered much of Europe under the great general Napoleon. The uniforms consisted of dark blue coats with red collars, cuffs, and shoulder boards; white trousers; and tall conical caps with a brass emblem on the front and trimmed with gold braid. Like the Texians, the main weapon of the Mexican soldiers was the musket. However, the Mexican musket had a bayonet—a long, pointed knife that fit below the musket's muzzle. The bayonet was used as a spear with which to stab an enemy in hand-to-hand combat.

A SHORT SIEGE, A SUDDEN ATTACK

General Santa Anna had not succeeded in catching the Texian force by surprise and destroying it in battle. Now he would have to put the Alamo under siege unless he could make the Texians surrender. He ordered some soldiers to take a large red flag up to the bell tower and hang it there, where the men in the fort could see it. This was a signal all soldiers recognized. It meant that unless the defenders of the Alamo surrendered immediately, all Texian and Tejano

Davy Crockett, center right with his rifle above his head, fighting during the attack on the Alamo.

soldiers would be killed. Once fighting started, no men in the Alamo would be allowed to surrender, no wounded men would be given aid or allowed to live.

Colonel Travis ordered a cannon to be fired. This was a way of telling Santa Anna that the men in the Alamo refused to surrender.

The siege began.

No sooner did it begin than Jim Bowie collapsed. It is not known what disease Bowie had come down with, but it was probably a form of pneumonia, generally fatal in those days. He was too weak to walk or even stand. He was taken into a small room near the Alamo's main gate and put on a

Courtyard of the Alamo in chaos during the attack

cot. He never got up again. He turned full command of the Alamo's forces over to Travis.

For days, Mexican cannons sent cannonballs thudding into the Alamo's walls and shells hurtling down to explode in the courtyard. The people in the Alamo kept hoping Travis's messages would bring help from nearby towns but no help came.

On March 4, Santa Anna called his officers together and asked for their opinions on whether or not to attack. Most of the officers were against it. The siege seemed to be working, so why launch an attack that could cost the lives of hundreds of soldiers? Why not just wait until starvation and despair forced the Alamo's defenders to give up? But the next day, Santa Anna ordered an attack for the following morning.

THE BATTLE FOR THE ALAMO

Before daybreak on the morning of March 6, the Mexican soldiers began lining up in battle formation. As the sky started to grow light, Santa Anna gave the order and a bugler sounded the call for attack. In those days every **regiment** of an army had a band that played march music as the regiment went into battle.

Dawn at the Alamo, a painting of the fighting that took place once the Mexicans broke through the gate.

Now the bands began to play, and with shouts and cheers the Mexican Army marched toward the Alamo. It moved in formations called attack columns. An attack column generally consisted of about six hundred men lined up in nine rows to form a big rectangle approximately 50 yards (45 m) wide and 20 yards (18 m) deep. However, Santa Anna's attack columns were only three to four hundred strong, and one had only one hundred men. Attack columns were sent against the Alamo from four directions.

Roused by the noise, the Alamo's defenders rushed to the walls. Colonel Travis dashed for the north wall, a shotgun in one hand and a saber in the other. He raced to the top of the ramp where the gunners were getting the cannon ready for a shot and fired a blast from his shotgun at the oncoming Mexican soldiers. An instant later, a ball from a Mexican musket struck him in the head. He was one of the first of the Alamo's defenders to be killed.

The three cannons on the north wall were loaded with scrap metal—nails, screws, pieces of horseshoes, and broken tools. When the cannons were fired, these objects were hurled out in a whirling, cone-shaped cloud that slammed into the clustered soldiers at the speed of a bullet. Men were horribly mangled and killed by the dozens. Texian soldiers also rained musket fire into the ranks of Mexicans from the top of the wall. Great gaps appeared in the attack column.

Attacks against the other walls had the same result. The Mexican soldiers scurried forward to huddle against the walls, where the cannons couldn't fire at them, and were unable to proceed any farther.

However, Santa Anna had kept some of his best troops back and now sent them forward against the north wall.

Jim Bowie was stabbed to death by Mexican soldiers while he lay ill on a cot.

DID ANY MAN ESCAPE FROM THE ALAMO?

According to legend, the night before the Mexican attack, Colonel Travis announced that if anyone wanted to try to leave, they could. It is said that one man, Louis Rose, managed to sneak through the Mexican lines and escape.

Many of the Texians on the top of the wall had been hit by Mexican musket fire, and there were now too few men to hold back this determined push. Mexican soldiers scrambled up ladders and swarmed onto the wall. The few Texians left jumped down into the courtyard and gathered together, firing as fast as they could at the horde of enemy soldiers coming at them. While some Mexicans fired back at the Texians and others charged at them with bayonets, a few ran to open the gate in the wall. More Mexican soldiers came pouring through the gate into the Alamo.

No one knows exactly what happened after this. A few Mexican soldiers and officers later described things they claimed to have seen, but some stories may have been made up.

According to one story, Davy Crockett and his twelve Tennessee sharpshooters stood with their backs to one corner of the wall, shooting down every group of soldiers that tried to rush them. One by one, the soldiers were all killed by musket fire.

Some Texians tried to escape by going over the wall, but Santa Anna had cavalrymen patrolling around the walls. All the Texians who tried to escape from the fort were caught and killed. The Texians who stayed in the fort ran into the rows of little rooms along the walls that were used as a barracks for lodging soldiers. They blocked the doors and knocked holes in the walls to fire their muskets through. Some ran into the church, blocked the door, and began shooting from the windows.

Mexican soldiers hauled cannons down from the walls and used them to blast open the doors to the barracks and the church. As soldiers burst into the rooms and the church, Texians and Tejanos fought them savagely with knives and tomahawks and used their muskets as clubs. One of the stories about Jim Bowie was that soldiers broke into the room where he lay on the cot holding two pistols. He fired both pistols, but the soldiers shot him in the head, and then bayoneted his dead body.

ANOTHER STORY ABOUT DAVY CROCKETT'S DEATH

One Mexican general insisted that Davy Crockett and the men with him surrendered. The general said he tried to save them, but Santa Anna himself ordered them killed and they were stabbed to death with swords.

Susannah Dickinson, one of the women who survived the siege of the Alamo

Eventually, every Texian and Tejano man who was in the Alamo that day was shot down or stabbed to death with bayonets. There were probably fewer than two hundred of them, but they fought so viciously that they killed or wounded between three hundred and five hundred Mexican soldiers.

"REMEMBER THE ALAMO!"

Two Texians did leave the Alamo alive. General Santa Anna let Captain Almeron Dickinson's wife, Susannah Dickinson, and her baby daughter, Angelina, leave the fort. The Tejana women and their children were also allowed to leave. So were two young African-American men known only as Joe and Ben, slaves of Colonel Travis and another Texian. The Mexicans knew they were slaves and had to do as they were told, so the Mexicans did not feel they should be punished in any way.

Mexican soldiers who had been killed were buried. The bodies of the Texians and Tejanos were burned. Santa Anna then led his army eastward, intending to wipe out all further resistance to the Mexican government.

News of what had happened at the Alamo quickly spread through Texas, carried by the women who had been allowed to leave. Texians became determined to have vengeance for all the men who had been slaughtered without being allowed to surrender. Men flocked to join General Houston's army.

On April 21, Santa Anna located Houston's army of about nine hundred Texians and Tejanos near the San Jacinto River. Santa Anna had about twelve hundred men and believed he had the Texians trapped and outnumbered. However, the Mexican soldiers were worn-out from a long march and a night without sleep. Santa Anna foolishly let them make camp less than a mile from Houston's force and go to sleep.

At 4:30 that afternoon, Houston's force attacked. Yelling "Remember the Alamo," they charged into the camp, catching the Mexicans by surprise. They now had bayonets on their rifles and they used them viciously. The Mexican army was shattered. Six hundred and fifty men were killed or wounded and most of the others taken prisoner. Santa Anna

The wounded General Houston (lying down) receives the surrendering Santa Anna

THE RESULT OF THE MEXICAN WAR

As a result of the Mexican War, 1846–1848, Mexico had

to sell the United States some of its

territory beyond Texas. In time, this territory became

the states of New Mexico, Arizona, California, Nevada,

Utah, and part of Colorado.

**The United States grew
following the Mexican War.**

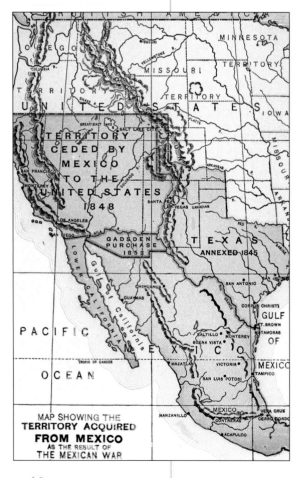

escaped by hiding in a swamp but was captured the next day. At General Houston's demand, Santa Anna signed a document stating that Texas was now free. He was allowed to return to Mexico, but there he was forced to give up the presidency.

On March 2, while the siege of the Alamo was still going on, the Texian leaders had declared that Texas was an independent nation—the Republic of Texas. After the Battle of San Jacinto there was an election for president of the republic, with Stephen F. Austin and Sam Houston on the ballot. Houston was elected first president of the Republic of Texas.

However, most Texians really wanted to become part of the United States, and most Americans wanted this, too. In 1845, by a vote of the U.S. Congress, Texas was admitted to the Union as the twenty-eighth state.

However, the government of Mexico refused to agree that Texas no longer belonged to Mexico. It sent troops to the region along the Rio Grande, where they clashed with U.S. forces. In May 1846, the U.S. Congress declared war on Mexico.

The war lasted from 1846 to 1848. An American army invaded Mexico. After several battles, Mexican forces surrendered,

BALLENTINE · JOHN J. BAUGH · JOSEPH BAYLISS · JOHN BLAIR · SAMUEL C. BLAIR · WILLIAM BLAZEBY · JAMES BUTLER BONHAM · JAMES BOWIE · JESSE B. BOWMAN · DANIEL
LLIAM CLOUD · ROBERT COCHRAN · GEORGE WASHINGTON COTTLE · HENRY COURTMAN · LEMUEL CRAWFORD · DAVID CROCKETT · ROBERT CROSSMAN · DAVID P. CUMMINGS
S H. DILLARD · JAMES DIMPKINS · SHEROD J. DOVER · LEWIS DUEL · ANDREW DUVALT · CARLOS ESPALIER · GREGORIO ESPARZA · ROBERT EVANS · SAMUEL B. EVANS · JAMES L. EW
RARD GARRETT · JOHN E. GARVIN · JOHN E. GASTON · JAMES GEORGE · JOHN CALVIN GOODRICH · ALFRED CALVIN GRIMES · JOSE MARIA GUERRERO · JAMES C. GWIN · JAMES
HOLLAND · SAMUEL HOLLOWAY · WILLIAM D. HOWELL · WILLIAM D. JACKSON · THOMAS JACKSON · GREEN B. JAMESON · GORDON C. JENNINGS · LEWIS JOHNSON · JOHN JONES · JOHNNY

Statue commemorating the Alamo

and Mexico was forced to agree that Texas was part of the United States.

A portion of the Alamo still stands in the city of San Antonio—the little church and part of the barracks where the Alamo's defenders made their last stand. It is now a museum and a memorial to the courage of the Texians and Tejanos whose defense of that place helped create the Republic of Texas and a piece of history that all Americans can take pride in.

Glossary

barrel—the long metal tube of a musket, rifle, or cannon, from which the projectile is fired

breeches—short pants that fit tightly at the knee

dictator—a nation's ruler who has complete power

frontier—a wilderness region at the edge of a nation's official border

immigration—entering into a new country to settle there

militia—a military force that belongs to a state and is not part of the regular army

monastery—a building, or group of buildings, where monks live

pelt—the skin of an animal, including its fur or hair

regiment—a basic military unit with an established name and number (Regiments were grouped together to form an army.)

republic—a nation with a government run by representatives who are elected by its citizens and responsible to them

siege—a military tactic of surrounding a town or fort with troops in order to cut off supplies and reinforcements, thus forcing it to surrender

Timeline: The Alamo

1830

APRIL 6
The Mexican government passes a law forbidding further immigration into Texas from the United States. Many Texians begin to talk of independence.

1833

APRIL 1
General Antonio López de Santa Anna becomes president of Mexico.

1834

APRIL 24
Santa Anna sets aside the Mexican constitution and takes control of the entire Mexican government.

1835

SEPTEMBER 10
Sent by Santa Anna, Mexican General Martín de Cós enters Texas with an army of four hundred, heading for San Antonio.

OCTOBER 9
General Cós arrives at San Antonio

NOVEMBER 1
The Texian Army of the People, commanded by Stephen F. Austin, lays siege to Cós's forces in San Antonio.

NOVEMBER 12
Sam Houston is named general of the Texas army.

DECEMBER 5
The Army of the People attacks the Mexican force in San Antonio.

DECEMBER 9
General Cós surrenders San Antonio to the Army of the People.

DECEMBER 31
Santa Anna begins to assemble an army of more than 6,500 to march on Texas.

1836

JANUARY 19
Colonel Bowie arrives in San Antonio with thirty men to reinforce the eighty-eight men there. Bowie and Colonel Neill decide they can hold the Alamo against a Mexican attack.

FEBRUARY 3
Lieutenant Colonel Travis brings thirty men to San Antonio.

FEBRUARY 8
Davy Crockett and a group of men from Tennessee arrive in San Antonio.

FEBRUARY 23
Santa Anna's army reaches San Antonio. The Texian force prepares to defend the Alamo.

MARCH 6
The Mexicans attack the Alamo and capture it, taking heavy losses. All Texian and Tejano men in the Alamo are killed.

APRIL 21
Santa Anna's army is destroyed by Houston's Army of Texas at the Battle of San Jacinto.

SEPTEMBER 5
Sam Houston is elected first president of the Republic of Texas.

To Find Out More

BOOKS

Bredeson, Carmen. *The Battle of the Alamo: The Fight for Texas Territory.* Brookfield, CT: Millbrook Press, 1996.

Garland, Sherry. *Voices of the Alamo.* New York: Scholastic Inc., 2000.

Lace, William W. *The Alamo.* San Diego: Lucent Books, 1997.

Sonelu, Roy. *The Alamo in American History.* Berkeley Heights, NJ: Enslow Publishers, Inc., 1996.

ONLINE SITES

The Alamo
www.thealamo.org

The Alamo-Table of Contents
www.hotx.com/alamo/toc.html

Daughters of the Republic of Texas Library: Alamo History
www.drtl.org/history/index.asp

Index

Bold numbers indicate illustrations.

About the Author

Tom McGowen is a children's book author with a special interest in military history. He has written fourteen previous books in this area. His most recent books in the Cornerstones of Freedom Series are *The Battle of Cantigny* and *The Attack on Pearl Harbor.* Author of fifty-six fiction and non-fiction books for young readers, he has received the Children's Reading Round Table Annual Award for Outstanding Contributions to the Field of Children's Literature.